WILLIAM

ENGLAND'S PRINCE OF HEARTS

WILLIAM

ENGLAND'S PRINCE OF HEARTS

By Marie T. Morreale

A JOHN BOSWELL ASSOCIATES BOOK

**Andrews McMeel
Publishing**

Kansas City

www.andrewsmcmeel.com

Library of Congress Cataloging-in-
Publication Data on file
ISBN: 0-8362-7130-0

Cover and book design
by Charles Kreloff

ATTENTION SCHOOLS AND BUSINESSES
Andrews McMeel books are available at
quantity discounts with bulk purchase for
educational, business, or sales promotional
use. For information, please write to:
Special Sales Department, Andrews
McMeel Publishing, 4520 Main Street,
Kansas City, Missouri 64111.

DEDICATION

To real-life Florida princes—Brandon and
John Poynor

ACKNOWLEDGMENTS

The author would like to thank the
following people for their assistance in
the research and production of this book:

John Boswell
Patty Brown
Charles Kreloff
Mark Bego
Randi Reisfield

Contents

Introduction

He's not Leonardo DiCaprio yelling "I'm king of the world" at the bow of the *Titanic*. Yet, one day, he *will* be king of the British empire.

He's not a pop star like Michael Jackson whose music brings hundreds of thousands of people to their feet at concert arenas all over the world. But millions of people across the globe have shared the joys and pains of his life.

He's not Jonathan Taylor Thomas, the top fan-mail addressee of TV sitcom land. However, he's probably received more mail than all the teen idols of 1998 combined!

If you haven't guessed yet, *he* is William Arthur Philip Louis Mountbatten-Windsor, His Royal Highness Prince of Wales. And *he* is the first child of the once-upon-a-time fairy tale love story that captured the hearts and souls of the twentieth century.

William's father is Charles Philip Arthur George Mountbatten, eldest son of Great Britain's Queen Elizabeth II and Prince Philip Mountbatten, Duke of Edinburgh. This lineage makes Charles next in line to the British throne. William's mother was the late Princess Diana, who, at the age of fourteen when her father, John Althorp, assumed the official title of Earl of Spencer, became Lady Diana Spencer. She, too, was of noble background.

Charles was born and bred to become King of England. When he was born on November 14, 1948, the entire world took notice of the little prince. Though his younger siblings, Princess Anne, Prince Andrew, and Prince Edward, were also greeted with delight when they were born, it was Charles who remained directly in the spotlight. He was raised in the very traditional ways of the Royal Family. His early

Prince William visits the Burnaby High School in Vancouver, Canada, in March 1998.

childhood was a mixture of pomp and circumstance, official ceremonies, prim and proper nannies, and being tutored at home, Buckingham Palace. Eventually he went off to the proper schools—Cheam School, Gordonstoun in Scotland, and the University of Cambridge. Charles followed the royal tradition of joining the navy. When he wasn't busy with official duties, he could often be found hunting at his family's vacation home, Balmoral, in Scotland, horseback riding or playing polo. Charles was definitely the picture-perfect prince.

As Charles entered his thirties, it was expected he would find the appropriate woman to become his bride, the eventual Queen of England. The pressure was on— from his family and from the British public. Little did he know that he had already met his future bride, Diana Spencer. No one would have guessed of their future together the first time they met. After all Charles was then twenty-one and Diana was only eight years old! Diana was first introduced to Charles when he visited Sandringham, the Queen's country estate in Norfolk.

Diana Frances Spencer was born on July 1, 1961. Her father was John Althorp, who inherited his title Earl of Spencer when his father passed away. At the time of

Prince Charles and Princess Diana on their wedding day.

Diana's birth, he was the Viscount Althorp. Diana's mother was Frances Ruth Burke Roche. She, too, was of noble lineage. Diana had two older sisters, Sarah and Jane, and their father had hoped for a male heir. But when he saw the beautiful baby Diana, he announced she was a "perfect specimen." (The Earl got his male heir several years later when Diana's younger brother, Charles, was born.) The Spencers lived in Park House on the grounds of Sandringham, a privilege afforded them because of their royal ties.

In many ways Diana's early childhood was something of a fairy tale—she was wealthy, pampered, and protected. Then, when she was just six years old, her perfect world began to shatter. Her parents separated and proceeded into a very public and bitter divorce. Unfortunately, Diana got a taste of the British tabloid press early on when her parents divorced. Their breakup made gossip headlines everywhere and Diana was subjected to whispers and stares wherever she went.

As is tradition in England, the children remained with the titled parent, which in this case was their father. However, Diana, Sarah, Jane, and Charles did get to spend a lot of time in London with their mother and her second husband, Peter Shand-Kydd, the heir to a wallpaper fortune.

When Diana was fourteen years old, her grandfather died and her father became the eighth Earl of Spencer. It was then that he and the children moved to the family estate in Northamptonshire. Diana was officially known as Lady Diana Spencer and she entered the whirlwind life of the nobility. However, it wasn't an easy transition for Diana. She had spent her early girlhood as something of a tomboy. Her hair tied up in pigtails, Diana was more at home climbing trees, swimming, and rough-housing with her little brother, Charles, than eating tea and crumpets. In public, she was a bit shy and quiet and as she entered her preteen and teen years, she could often be found with her nose in a book written by the queen of the romance novels, Barbara Cartland. (Cartland, also, just happened to be Diana's step-grandmother!)

Diana attended elite boarding schools, but never really distinguished herself academically. As a matter of fact, one of her

Charles and Diana on their honeymoon at the royal palace at Balmoral, Scotland.

Three months after their wedding... Charles and Diana were expecting their first child.

school reports described her as "a girl who notices what needs to be done, then does it willingly and cheerfully."

Then, when Diana was sixteen years old, her future began to unfold. It was in the fall of 1977 and Diana had returned home from school for a weekend pheasant hunt and party. Prince Charles was to be the honored guest. At the time, he was dating Diana's older sister, Sarah. But when Charles was reintroduced to Diana, she was no longer the pig-tailed tomboy he had met years before. They first spoke in the middle of the field during the pheasant hunt and Charles recalled Diana as "a very jolly and amusing and attractive sixteen-year-old."

Though Charles and Sarah's relationship didn't last, they remained friendly and he asked her to attend his thirtieth birthday party at Buckingham Palace. Diana was also invited. That was in 1978. In 1979, Prince Andrew, Charles's brother, invited Diana to spend a summer vacation at Balmoral, the royal vacation estate in Scotland. By 1980, a true romance had blossomed between Charles and Diana, but the two tried to keep their relationship out of the tabloids. Charles would not admit to the press that he was seeing just one girl, and Diana would tell those who asked that she was seeing Charles Renfrew—Baron Renfrew is one of Charles's royal titles.

Eventually the deceptions couldn't hide the romance between Charles and Diana, and in September 1980, the first headlines began to appear about the couple. At the time, the eighteen-year-old Diana was a teacher at the Young England Kindergarten, but she resigned her position when Charles presented her with an eighteen-carat sapphire-and-diamond engagement ring in February 1981.

Diana was the perfect choice for Charles. She was beautiful, from the nobility, and obviously totally devoted to him. She moved into Buckingham Palace so she could plan what would come to be known as "the wedding of the century."

The months before a wedding are full of pressures for any bride, but Diana faced a world she had only tasted when her parents divorced: the Tabloid Press Jungle. After leading a life generally out of the spotlight, Diana was suddenly surrounded by reporters and photographers wherever she went. The shy Diana was chased and hounded by the press and she often dissolved into tears. But despite her frazzled nerves and hide-and-seek relationship with the press, Diana was also becoming a poised princess.

The entire world saw her complete transformation on July 29, 1981, when Diana and Charles walked down the aisle at St. Paul's Cathedral and were married by the Archbishop of Canterbury. There were almost 3,000 guests at the wedding and an additional 750 million people watched the wedding on television all over the world. At the reception the festivities began when Charles, who was dressed in his Commander of the Royal Navy uniform, made the first slice of the five-foot-high, 200-pound wedding cake with his ceremonial saber.

William at age eight trying out his Christmas present, a shiny new BMX bike.

The Archbishop of Canterbury's words as he introduced the newlyweds summed up what everyone was thinking—and hoping. "Here is the stuff of which fairy tales are made: the Prince and Princess on their wedding day."

The fairy tale continued as the couple spent a fourteen-day honeymoon sailing the Mediterranean on the royal yacht *Britannia*. The newshounds didn't give the royal couple a break even on their honeymoon, but Charles and Diana seemed to have eyes only for each other. Romance was in the air. When they returned to England, they settled into two official residences: Kensington Palace in London and a country estate called Highgrove in Gloucestershire. Diana was thrown into the fast-paced life of a princess. Not only did she have to set up two households, write thank-you notes for more than 10,000 wedding gifts (her secretary helped, of course!), and participate in the official ceremonies and duties of the Royal Family, but she also had to adapt to married life. Diana did that quite well. Three months after their wedding, Buckingham Palace announced that Charles and Diana were expecting their first child.

Prince of Wails

At 9:03 P.M., June 21, 1982, Charles and Diana, the Prince and Princess of Wales, became the proud parents of a seven pound, one-and-a-half ounce baby boy. After seventeen hours of labor, the baby was born at St. Mary's Hospital in the Paddington section of London. Charles had been at Diana's bedside the entire time and was there to see his baby son at the moment of delivery. Indeed, the baby's arrival was quite different from his father's,

When William gets fussy at his christening, Diana quiets him by letting him suck her finger as Charles looks on.

Nanny Barbara Barnes carries her charge, nine-month-old William, from the plane on his first royal trip to Australia. The residents of "Down Under" loved baby Wills and nicknamed him "Willie Wombat."

since Charles had been born at Buckingham Palace with his father, Prince Philip, doing the expectant father's pace outside the royal birthing rooms. It had been tradition for royal births to occur at "home" instead of a hospital, but in 1974 it was decided that St. Mary's would be the site of all future royal births.

The official birth announcement said simply, "The Princess of Wales was safely delivered of a son at 9:03 P.M. today. Her Royal Highness and her child are doing well."

At first the baby was known only as "Baby of Wales," because Diana and Charles were still "discussing" what to name their son!

When Charles emerged from St. Mary's, he was surrounded by the press, all calling out questions. *New York Post* reporter Harry Arnold asked the Prince how it went. Smiling broadly, the usually staid Charles replied: "Nearly seventeen hours is a long time to wait. Obviously I'm relieved, delighted....I think it's marvelous. It's a rather grown-up thing, I've found. It's rather a shock."

When asked if the baby had hair, Charles answered, "It's blond, sort of fairish." Someone else yelled out, "Does he look like his dad?" And Charles laughed. "No! He's lucky enough not to."

Then came the question about the baby's name and Charles responded, "We have a few names in mind. You'll have to ask my wife about that. There is an argument about it." Reportedly, Charles wanted to name him Arthur, and Diana wanted to name their son William. Diana eventually won this "argument" and several weeks later the baby was officially named William Arthur Philip Louis

Playtime in the royal quarters at Kensington Palace for Charles, Diana, and baby William.

At first the baby was known only as "Baby of Wales," because Diana and Charles were still "discussing" what to name their son!

Diana and her children, Wills and baby Harry, otherwise known as "The Heir and a Spare."

Mountbatten-Windsor.

Oh, yes, there was one last question for Charles before he left the hospital. A reporter asked when Charles and Diana were going to have another baby! After a moment, Charles replied, "You'll have to ask my wife about that...." And then he seemed to hesitate another moment and laughingly said, "Bloody hell, give us a chance!"

Charles and Diana with their bouncing baby boy, Wills.

The entire British population laughed with their Prince, and celebrated. A forty-one gun salute echoed from the guns of the Royal Horse Artillery troop in Hyde Park shortly after the birth announcement was made. All over the country church bells—from St. Paul's Cathedral to the smallest village house of prayer—rang out in joy. Great Britain not only had a future King in Charles, but a King-in-waiting with the birth of William. The royal succession was safe and secure.

Back at Kensington Palace, all was being made ready for Diana and the baby's return. The royal nursery, decorated by the famous designer Dudly Poplak, was fit for a king . . . at least a prince. The baby's crib had a full canopy and the linens matched its rosebud print. Gifts from family members and heads of state all over the world lined the shelves. Everything was ready for William.

When the little prince was placed in his crib, it was reported that he "lustily" pronounced his approval! Indeed, anyone close to the royal nursery would attest to the fact that baby William, who Princess Diana had nicknamed Wills, had a healthy set of lungs.

The press was let in on the secret of Wills's early verbalizations when they next officially saw him—at his christening on August 4, 1982. That day was also the eighty-second birthday of William's paternal great-grandmother, affectionately known as the Queen Mum. It was a day of great celebration. Following royal tradition, William's christening outfit was the Honiton lace robes originally made for Edward VII in 1842.

The actual christening took place in the music room at

Kensington Palace. It was performed by the Archbishop of Canterbury, the same reverend who had married Charles and Diana. During the twenty-five-minute ceremony, the Archbishop baptized William with water from the Jordan River, a tradition that dates back to the Crusades. The baby was sponsored by six official godparents, close friends and family members of Charles and Diana's. The little group included Sir Laurens van der Post, an author and best friend of Prince Charles; Princess Alexandra; the Duchess of Westminster; Lady Susan Hussey, a lady-in-waiting to Queen Elizabeth II; the ex-monarch of Greece, King Constantine; and Lord Romsey.

During the ceremony, William was quite vocal, leading the press to dub him "Prince of Wails."

Home Is Where the Heart Is

The baby gifts continued to pour in—both at Kensington Palace and the Wales country estate, Highgrove. Obviously there were more things arriving than Wills could ever use, so Diana donated many of the gifts to children's hospitals and orphanages. That act was just a precursor of Diana's desire to reach out and help those in need—a trait she was determined to pass on to Wills and any other children she had.

Though Diana was a definite hands-on mom, the day-to-day duties of taking care of Wills were relegated to a nanny. Barbara Barnes was hired by Diana and Charles after friends had recommended her. She was a breath of fresh air. Barbara, as she preferred to be called, didn't wear the traditional starchy white uniform and she had a gentle approach to her charge. She was assisted by another nanny, Olga Powell.

Part of Charles and Diana's official duties often required them to travel around the world. However, Diana was determined to be a full-time mother and she was

Charles and Diana enjoy a day on the palace grounds with Wills.

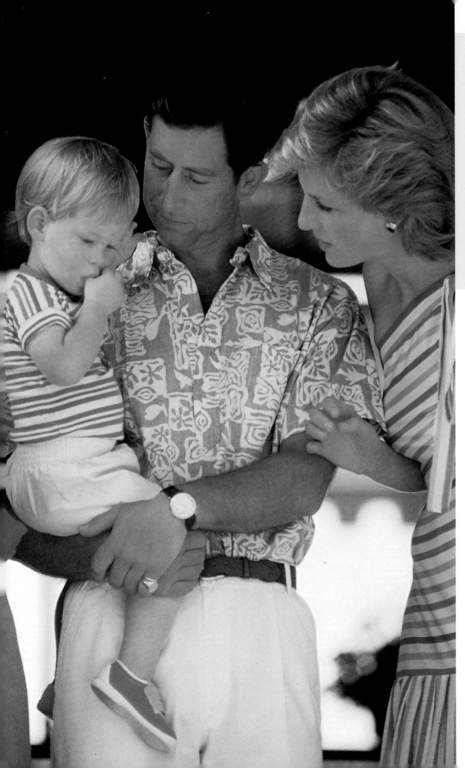

"William is not at all shy. He's a great grinner, but he does dribble a lot."

able to put off many trips during Wills's first year. Though the press seemed insatiable when it came to news of Prince William and were clamoring for photo opportunities, Diana and Charles decided that they would very carefully control what was released. When Wills was three months old, he sat for his first official photo, which was shot by his great-uncle, Lord Snowden, who was the husband of Queen Elizabeth's sister, Princess Margaret.

The next time Wills was photographed was shortly before his first Christmas. Carefully selected photographers were allowed to shoot him at Kensington Palace. The six-month-old William performed masterfully, smiling and gurgling throughout the entire photo shoot. Proud papa Charles

Charles showing off his hands-on fatherhood with Wills as Diana looks on.

Wills gives his first press conference!

practically crowed as his seventeen-pound bouncing baby boy, whom he had dubbed "Willie Wombat," won the hearts of all who met him. "He's wonderful fun and really makes you laugh," Charles said of his son. "He's not at all shy. He's a great grinner, but he does dribble a lot."

At nine months, William accompanied his parents on his first state trip. It was a good-will trip to Australia and New Zealand. This six-week journey was part of Charles and Diana's official duties, but before them, no other young royal couple thought of bringing an infant child with them. Diana would hear of nothing but!

Though it was reported that Queen Elizabeth was not enthusiastic about the idea of Wills accompanying Charles and Diana, she finally gave her royal blessing. The Queen's objections to Wills going with his parents were twofold. It was just against tradition, but most importantly there was the royal custom that two heirs to the throne would never travel together for fear of an accident. However, Diana persevered and some believed it was because she pointed out that it would be a good "political" move for the British subjects of Australia to meet their baby prince up close and personal.

Whether it was the politics of it or Diana's desire not to be separated from her son, it was the correct move. Australia and New Zealand fell in love with the prince, who had been nicknamed

Prince William was exposed to his royal duties early on. Here, three-year-old Wills, with the Queen Mother, Queen Elizabeth, and Prince Philip, waves to the British public from a balcony at Buckingham Palace.

by the Down-Under press "Billy the Kid."

Upon the Royal Family's return to England, the press continued their trolling for any and all news about baby Wills. The most was made of the official photo sessions and announcements that came from the Palace. Wills's each infant landmark was chronicled by newspapers, TV reporters, and magazines. One such publication, *Royalty* magazine, published the following description of Wills's progress:

"He could smile at six weeks, roll onto his tummy and support his upper body on his forearms at seventeen weeks; sit with support at six months, and sit without support shortly afterward. His first tooth peeked out at eight months; he crawled at nine months and took his first steps at ten months, supported by 'Jumbo,' his father's old blue elephant on wheels. He took his first unaided steps at Highgrove and weighed twenty-five pounds at his first birthday."

By the time Wills was a toddler, he had won the hearts of an entire nation, even the world!

Royal Residences: The Many Homes of Wills

BUCKINGHAM PALACE: Probably the most famous royal residence, Buckingham Palace is the Queen's official London home. Originally called Buckingham House, it was the London home of the Dukes of Buckingham. In 1762 it was bought by King George III, who moved there with Queen Charlotte. George IV, who became King in 1820, hired architect John Nash to turn Buckingham House into a state palace. At George IV's death, Nash was dismissed and Buckingham was not finished until the reign of Queen Victoria, who was the first royal actually to live at the Palace. Architect Edward Blore took on the duties of expanding Buckingham Palace, and finally in 1913, designer Aston Webb refaced the Palace facade with Portland stone. This is the Buckingham Palace we know today.

WINDSOR CASTLE: More than 900 years ago, William the Conqueror chose the site for Windsor Castle. Set high above the Thames River, it was a day's

A four-year-old Prince William visits a police headquarters and takes over.

Changing of the Guard at Buckingham Palace.

march from the Tower of London. Windsor was intended to be the western guardian to London. Since those early days, Windsor has been an official royal residence. Over the years, various sovereigns improved and added to Windsor and to this day it has important traditions connected to it. Windsor's State Apartments are the formal rooms used for official ceremonies and occasions, for both the royal Court and the government. The rooms show off some of the most valuable works of art in the Royal Collection, including paintings by Rembrandt, Rubens, Holbein, and van Dyck. Also within Windsor

stands St. George's Chapel, which was started in 1475 by Edward IV and completed by Henry VIII.

ST. JAMES PALACE: This palace was built between 1532 and 1540 by Henry VIII and is the oldest of the royal residences that was home to the reigning Sovereign and his or her Court. St. James is where foreign Ambassadors are presented to the Court and High Commissions are accredited. (It is at St. James that such celebrities as Paul McCartney and Elton John received the official title of "Sir.") Though it still remains the official residence of the Sovereign, the kings and queens of England have had their main residence in Buckingham Palace since 1837. St. James Palace is the London residence of the Prince of Wales, and since Diana's death Princes William and Harry have joined their father, Prince Charles, there. It also includes Clarence House, the London home of Queen Elizabeth, the Queen Mother, and Lancaster House, which is used for government conferences and receptions.

St. James Palace

KENSINGTON PALACE: Originally known as Nottingham House, William III bought the residence from the Earl of Nottingham in 1689. William III commissioned the outstanding architect of the day, Christopher Wren, to renovate and extend the residence. Until the death of King George II in 1760, Kensington Palace was one of the Sovereign's favorite homes. Queen Victoria was born and brought up in Kensington. However, when she ascended to the throne, she moved to Buckingham Palace and never again stayed at Kensington. Today Kensington houses the offices and residence of Princess Margaret, sister of Queen Elizabeth II; Princess Alice and the Duke and Duchess of Gloucester; the Duke and Duchess of Kent; and Prince and Princess Michael of Kent. Kensington also used to be the home of Princess Diana.

SANDRINGHAM HOUSE: Originally bought in 1862 for the Prince of Wales, (later King Edward VII), Sandringham has been a private home for sovereigns for four generations. The Queen and members of the Royal Family always spend Christmas at Sandringham and stay there until February of each

Balmoral Castle in Scotland.

year. The Sandringham Estate, nearly 20,000 acres, is a commercial entity run by the Land Agent for the Queen. Half of the estate is rented out to tenant farmers, while the rest holds an official sawmill run by the Department of Forestry, two horse stud farms, a fruit farm, and a country park. Also on the estate is Sandringham Country Park. Over 600 acres and open to the public for free all year long, the park has camping sites and nature trails, and hosts many craft fairs and country shows throughout the year.

BALMORAL CASTLE: Built in the fifteenth century, Scotland's Balmoral Castle was originally bought for Queen Victoria by her husband, Prince Albert, in 1852. At the time it was determined that the original castle was too small

and Prince Albert planned and designed a new castle himself. It was finished in 1855. Over the years, successive generations of Royals made improvements to the castle. Today Balmoral Estate consists of more than 50,000 acres of hill country, forests, and small tenant farms. It also includes a game reserve and is Prince Charles's favorite vacation residence. He loves to hike and hunt on the grounds of Balmoral. After the tragic death of Princess Diana, Prince Charles brought Princes William and Harry to Balmoral for the days preceding her funeral. He knew they needed to be out of the spotlight of the press at that time and Balmoral was the perfect retreat.

Prince or Wild Child?

Prince William directs the Royal Family photo at Prince Harry's christening.

Wills was definitely a darling, but as he reached those "terrible twos," he entered what those close to him called "a phase." The press picked up on Wills's tendency to express himself—anywhere, anytime. He had even earned another nickname: "Billy the Basher."

One of Prince Charles's favorite duties was bathing little Wills, but as the little prince began exercising his independence, things changed. As reporter Barry Hillenbrand wrote in an article for *Time* magazine back then, "the bathroom became a war room. Wills started breaking things [and] flushing his father's shoes down the toilet."

The Royal Family takes a bike ride.

Indeed, his father's shoes had a definite attraction for Wills. Another of Wills's favorite tricks was hiding golf balls in Charles's carefully stored shoes and letting out peals of laughter when his father attempted to put them on. Of course, Wills *didn't* make anyone laugh the times he accidentally set off the security alarms in the royal residences. But then, boys will be boys!

Here Comes Harry

Shortly after Wills celebrated his second birthday, Princess Diana gave birth to his little brother. It was at 4:20 A.M. on September 15, 1984, and the blessed event again took place at St. Mary's Hospital. The baby weighed in at six

pounds, fourteen ounces and was officially named Prince Henry Charles Albert David Mountbatten-Windsor. He was immediately nicknamed "Harry," though the press sometimes called him "The Spare." This shortened version of the phrase "An Heir and a Spare" referred to the fact that Charles and Diana already had an heir in Wills, but if something happened to him,

Harry would be next in line.

The day after Harry was born, Wills and Charles went to the hospital for the baby's first official visit. A crowd of thousands of well-wishers had gathered outside the hospital and as Wills and Charles entered they were greeted with cheers. When Wills walked into Diana's room, he immediately rushed into his mother's arms. And when he was introduced to his little brother, he broke out in smiles and giggles. According to Prince Charles, Wills and Harry "got along beautifully, right from the first moment."

Actually, Harry was a ready-made audience for and participant in Wills's mischievous adventures. Whether it was the trail of broken toys Wills left in his wake or the photos of him saluting his father in imitation of the royal troops at official ceremonies, Harry always seemed to be sharing the fun with his older brother. Another thing Wills and Harry shared was their mother's overwhelming love. It was obvious to those who were close to the Royal Family, as well as to ordinary citizens, that Diana had a special relationship with her sons. She was definitely a presence in their lives. Though nannies, butlers, valets, chauffeurs, secretaries, housekeepers, cooks, and even bodyguards surrounded the little princes on a daily basis, Diana was their solid foundation. Early on she had determined that her children were not going to be raised in the lonely, stiff-upper-lip tradition that was accepted by royals—even by Prince Charles when he was a child.

This is not to say that Charles was a distant father, but as the heir to the throne, he had many duties that took him away from home. When Diana had to travel with Charles, she tried to take Wills and Harry along. However, there were many times that Charles was away from his family for weeks at a time.

Charles also had a knack for stirring up controversy even when he was at home. He loved to play polo or go hunting and riding at Balmoral and sometimes he would take off on his own. Even after Charles had brought Diana and Harry home from the hospital, he made headlines. Only hours after they returned to Kensington Palace, Charles took off for a polo match with his friends. The resulting whispers weren't the first time, nor would they be the last, that Charles was called an "absentee father."

Even when Wills became a handful, Diana could make things all right.

"Hugs can do a great amount of good, especially for children," Diana once said.

Diana, however, was determined to keep things perfect for her children. She was trying to live up to the "fairy tale" life everyone imagined she was leading. Her main concern was that, though Wills and Harry had to learn and accept certain traditions and duties as princes, she wanted her sons to grow up as "normal" as possible.

She didn't want them to be raised in the cloistered atmosphere that their father had. She wanted them to experience everything from amusement parks to fast-food restaurants to public playgrounds to real schools. Diana wanted her sons to have playmates. Having been a kindergarten teacher, Diana knew the importance of early social interaction for children. Luckily there were some ready-made playmates for Wills and Harry. His cousin Peter Phillips, the son of Charles's sister Princess Anne, was one of Wills's buddies, and he still is to this day. Peter, who is a little older than Wills, reportedly taught him that wonderful childish trick: stick out your tongue every time a camera is around! Wills was also close to Peter's sister, Zara. She is a year older than Wills, but reportedly loved to "mother" him and little Harry.

Life Inside the Palace

Diana tried to keep things as smooth and comfortable as possible. She wanted little change in their lives. But there were times when Diana instigated the change herself. Reportedly, there were those who felt that the nanny, Barbara Barnes, was a bit indulgent with the children and let Wills run a little wild. He was quickly becoming known as a tiny terror. Some say she was replaced by a new nanny, Ruth Wallace, because of that. Ruth (or "Roof" as Harry called her) was said to be a bit sterner than Nanny Barnes.

The new nanny, however, didn't seem able to tame Wills totally either, and as he went from being a toddler to a little boy, the tales of his antics added up. When

"The bathroom became a war room. Wills started breaking things [and] flushing his father's shoes down the toilet."

Wills was four years old, for example, he was a page boy at the wedding of his Uncle Andrew and Sarah Ferguson. Dressed in a sailor suit—very reminiscent of the outfit his father Charles wore at official ceremonies when he was a little boy—Wills seemed to have it in for the little girls at the ceremony. He made faces at the girls who gave flowers to his grandmother, the Queen; he stuck out his tongue (thank you, Peter!) at little girls who were at the church; and he even got into what has been described as a "mite-size fight" with a flower girl.

Though the world loved little Wills, he wasn't exactly making friends and influencing people in his inner circle. Again when he was four years old, he made a trip to the Royal Highland Fusiliers, an elite group of soldiers. From early on, Wills had a fascination with the pageantry of soldiers in dress uniform. He liked to mimic them standing at attention and saluting his father. But during this visit, Wills reportedly was a little full of himself and ordered the soldiers around. Supposedly he even threatened to fire them and let out a royal wail when they ignored him!

William and Harry loved doing "normal" kid things with Diana—like visiting the circus.

Prince William signs an official book at a royal ceremony.

Another legendary tale recalls the time he went to a friend's birthday party and ended up turning the festivity into a food fight. When he was reprimanded, it was reported that he drew himself up and asked in his best regal voice, "Do you know who I am?"

Wills was five when he attended another birthday party, and according to some insiders, he threw a tantrum when he couldn't blow out the candles on the cake.

Princes Harry and William show off their new Wetherby School uniforms for their mom, Princess Diana, and teacher Frederika Blair Turner.

But that wasn't all. Reportedly, when Wills was packed off to go home, he left with the Henry VIII-style remark that when he grew up and was King, he would send his knights to chop off their heads!

Things started to settle down a bit after Wills had been in nursery school for a while. At first, the subject of Wills's education was a major palace controversy. Diana and Charles didn't want their children to be tutored at home, but Queen Elizabeth came up with a compromise: start a nursery school at Kensington Palace and have other children come there.

Finally Diana and Charles prevailed and on September 24, 1985, the three-year-old Prince William went to Mrs. Mynors's Nursery School. The headmistress, Jayne Mynors, was the sister-in-law of a cousin of the Queen Mother and had established a very successful nursery school located in the Nottinghill Gate section of West London. Diana and Charles brought Wills to school that first day and as he kissed them good-bye, it was obvious he was anxious to get inside and see what was going on. Inside were thirty-five other children, divided by age into

The Windsor Princes—Harry, Charles, and William.

called "Prince of Wails" he was more often referred to as "William the Wonderful." When William was four and a half, he left Mrs. Mynors's Nursery School and enrolled in Wetherby School, a pre-prep school that prepared its students for their future education as well as life in society. Wills was in a class of twenty boys. Their academic studies included reading, writing, arithmetic, and geography. Their cultural studies included French and art. Will loved the art classes, but here he definitely expressed his early love of the military pomp. While other boys were drawing cars and trucks, he was creating castles with battles going on.

Wills was initially placed in the less-advanced group of his class, a form called Three Red. This did not bother Charles and Diana, since they were most concerned with Wills learning to fit in. Charles even told a *Time* magazine reporter: "Being too bright can be a positive disadvantage for the sort of life that William has before him. We're open-minded about William and his education. I would like to try and bring up our children to be well mannered, to think of other people, to put themselves in other people's positions. That way, if they

groups: the Cygnets, the Little Swans, and the Big Swans. Wills was first assigned to the Cygnets. He spent his days learning how to draw and work with clay, playing games, and listening to music.

Mostly he learned how to interact with other children.

After a year and a half with Mrs. Mynors, Wills had definitely begun to calm down. He still had his moments, but instead of being turn out not to be very bright or very qualified, at least if they have reasonable manners, they will get so much further in life than if they did not have any at all."

As it turned out, Charles didn't have to worry about William not being too bright. Wetherby seemed to challenge Wills's natural inquisitiveness and his grades reflected it.

Another thing that interested Wills was computers, and he distinguished himself by composing prose on-screen that included "naughty" words such as *wee* and *bottom*, which he spelled "botem."

But Wills really began to flourish at Wetherby and became quite popular there. There was, however, still a touch of the old "Wombat" that reared up every so often. "Prince William can be a really bossy-boots," a mother of one of his classmates at the time told *People* magazine. "I suppose it shouldn't be surprising. But he is a natural leader and likes to take command. He likes to organize games of tag that can get quite boisterous."

But the sensitive side of William was also flourishing. Another classmate's mother told a reporter: "I've often seen Prince William comforting a young child who's clearly unhappy. He'll talk

"Prince William is a natural leader and likes to take command."

earnestly to him and make sure he's all right before resuming playing. He really does think of others."

William inherited his sensitive nature from his mother, Princess Diana. As the years passed, many would observe how much he was becoming like her—not only in looks but also in temperament. William became very protective of his little brother, Harry. Indeed, Harry was a bit shyer than Wills was, and there were times he needed a big brother. Ironically, there were also times when Harry acted up—much like Wills used to—and it was big brother who calmed the situation down. The perfect example is the day Diana brought Harry and Wills to visit their Aunt Fergy, who had just given birth to their cousin Beatrice. Fergy was in Portland Hospital, and the usual crowd of

Wills got the "royal wave" down pat early on.

Boys will be boys—even at Wetherby School. Wills enjoys a little rough housing with his classmates under the watchful eye of Sergeant Cracker.

photographers were lined up outside to get their photos. When the Royal Family left the hospital, the rush of press surged toward them, and Harry stuck his tongue out at them. "Stop it, Harry," hissed Wills. "That's very naughty."

In 1990, Wills began his academic career at Ludgrove, an exclusive prep school in Workingham, only twenty-five miles from London. At first there was speculation that Wills would attend St. Paul's, a day school in West London. Supposedly Diana wasn't quite ready to let him go to boarding school, but she finally agreed to Ludgrove. William would board during the week and on Friday he would return home to his family. This suited Princess Diana just fine since her darling first-born wasn't *too* far away. That was important to her because by this time, it was obvious to her that her fairy tale marriage was crumbling.

Growing Up in the Spotlight

Whether or not Wills was completely aware of his parents' problems at the time, no one knows. But one thing is sure: he had already begun to be wary in front of the press. No longer was he waving, preening, or even acting up in front of photographers. Wills had already started copying his mother's shy downward stare when he was out in public.

When Diana and Charles brought Wills to Ludgrove, it was almost a strategic military move. Diana and Wills left their home together in one car. Charles left from a different location in another car. At a predetermined short distance from Ludgrove, the two cars met up and Diana and Wills joined Charles in his vehicle. Only then did they drive on to the grounds of Ludgrove—the perfect family. When Wills bid his parents good-bye at the front steps of the school, he didn't even look at the photojournalists straining to get a shot or hear a comment. What the press did get was shots of Diana and Charles standing on either side of Prince William as the boy shook hands with the headmaster, Gerald Barber, and his wife, Janet, and disappeared into the front doors of Ludgrove.

Wills fit in well at Ludgrove and was treated just like the rest of the students—as much as possible, at least. Of course, none of the other boys had bodyguards and electronic security devices, but as far as classes and extracurricular activities were concerned, Prince William was just one of the boys.

Princes Harry and William tell Santa their Christmas wishes.

He shared a room with four other boys and had to endure the typical low-man-on-the-totem-pole attitude the older students had toward newcomers. First-year students were called "squits" by the upperclassmen. Wills wore the official blue Ludgrove uniform, shared a communal bathroom, and went to classes—just like everyone else. He awoke at 7:15 A. M. and obeyed the 8:00 P. M. "lights out" rule.

Prince William also participated in a number of the sports offered at Ludgrove, such as swimming, tennis, and golf. Diana was always there when Wills was in a competition; she even played doubles with him at a mother-son tennis tournament. After that fun-filled day, Prince William proved his manners were definitely being polished—the nine-year-old made dinner reservations for himself and Diana that night at her favorite restaurant, San Lorenzo.

There were still moments that the old "Wild Willie" personality reared its mischievous head, like the time a photographer actually caught the nine-year-old prince trying to pinch the rear end of a

As Princess Diana looks on approvingly, Prince William accepts flowers from some loving British citizens.

pretty teacher! You better believe Diana had some strong words for her son after that!

But mostly, Diana was always there to comfort her first-born. One of the best-remembered incidents of Diana "being there" for Prince William was June 3, 1991, when he was rushed to the hospital after being hit in the head with a golf club. It seems that Wills and a classmate were fooling around on Ludgrove's golf putting green. According to an observer of the incident: "One lad started swinging a putter around his head. William happened to be in the way."

Prince William's security guards immediately went into overdrive. Wills was rushed to the hospital in a police car, as his Royal Protection Squad detective phoned the Palace with the code phrase "Operation Prince." That meant there was an emergency with Prince William. Diana also received a call from Ludgrove's headmaster. She was at Kensington Palace and immediately jumped into her Jaguar and drove herself straight to the hospital near Ludgrove. Prince Charles was notified at his rooms at Highgrove, and he too headed for Workingham. Though they arrived separately, Charles and

Diana formed a united front to comfort their little boy. Wills got a CAT scan and it was determined that he had a depressed fracture of the skull on his upper left forehead. He was then transferred to the Great Ormond Street Hospital in London and underwent an operation to repair the damage and check to see if there were any internal injuries. The procedure, conducted by neurosurgeon Richard Hayward, took a little over an hour and was announced to be a "complete success."

Diana had ridden in the ambulance with Wills when they brought him from Workingham to London. She was right there when Wills was rolled into the recovery room. And she spent the next two days and nights with her son at the hospital until he was released and allowed to go home.

The problem was with Charles. Though he was obviously concerned about his son, Charles had official duties to tend to. He knew his son was in good hands, so Charles left the hospital even before the surgery. He was scheduled to attend a performance of *Tosca* at the Royal Opera House with several government officials that night. When he

Prince Harry likes to carry his own bags!

arrived at the performance, he reassured everyone that Prince William was doing well. When the press realized that Prince Charles had left the hospital before Wills's operation, they voiced their ire in headlines. And when Prince Charles continued with his duties the next day and didn't visit Wills in the hospital until the next night, he was blasted once again. "What Kind Of Dad Are You?" asked the mega-size headlines of the *Sun*, one of London's most-read newspapers.

The fact that more and more people had begun to realize that Diana and Charles were living in separate residences made Charles's frequent absences from his sons' lives seem even worse. Some tabloids even called him a "delinquent dad" since it seemed his royal duties, as well as polo games and social commitments, kept him from spending time with his children. Meanwhile, Diana was *always* there. She picked up Wills at school every Friday and took him home to Kensington Palace for the weekends. Even on some special holidays, Charles pulled a no-show. Yet Diana was always there.

Diana joins Princes William and Harry at the annual School Sports Day at Ludgrove.

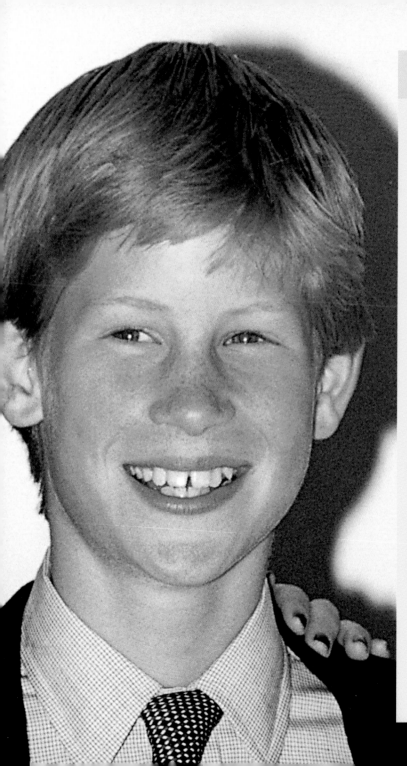

PRINCE HARRY FACT FILE

FULL NAME: Prince Henry Charles Albert David Mountbatten–Windsor

NICKNAME: Harry

OFFICIAL TITLE: His Royal Highness Prince Henry of Wales

BIRTHDATE: September 15, 1984, at 4:20 A.M.

BIRTHPLACE: St. Mary's Hospital in Paddington, London

ASTROLOGICAL SIGN: Virgo

CHRISTENING: December 21, 1984, at St. George Chapel

HEIGHT: 5'4"

WEIGHT: 110 pounds

HAIR: Reddish blond

EYES: Blue

PRESENT SCHOOL: Ludgrove

FUTURE SCHOOL: Eton—at first it was decided that Harry would attend Radley, but Charles changed his mind and felt that it would be good for Harry to be at school with his older brother.

13TH-BIRTHDAY PRESENT: A computer play station (Diana promised it to him, but her sister Lady Sarah McCorquodale gave it to him.)

FAVE FOODS: Junk food, chocolate

FAVE DRINK: Coke

FAVE FEMALE CELEBRITY: Cindy Crawford

FAVE SPICE GIRL: Emma "Baby Spice" Bunton

FAVE HOBBIES: Enjoys studying botany

FAVE SPORTS: Skiing, horseback riding, and snowboarding

FAVE VIDEO GAME: Sonic the Hedgehog

School Days

William in his Eton uniform.

As Wills was getting into the swing of things at boarding school, things were really changing on the home front. Though it was not official, Princess Diana and Prince Charles had all but completely separated. Because of this and Charles's royal duties, this also meant he was less present in his sons' lives. Those who had grown up with Charles didn't see much wrong with the situation, and one friend of the Prince explained, "Charles is treating William pretty much the same way his own father, Philip, treated Charles." Another friend, coming to Charles's defense, added: "When [Charles] does see the boys, he's all over them. But then, he might not choose to see them again for a month or so." And even author Brian Hoey, who has written some thirteen books on the Windsor Royal Family, supported the fact that Charles was essentially a good dad, saying: "[The press] always used to say Diana

Prince William with Head Master Andrew Gailey, who is in charge of the Prince's dorm, Manor House.

was the tactile one, but privately Charles also was. He used to kiss the boys good night and bathe them when they were little—which no father of the Royal Family has done in centuries."

And even Diana's friend Peter Archer wrote of Charles: "He is the heir, and he had to be away from home. This is the way of aristocrats. They don't see as much of their children as an ordinary British family, but that's not to say he doesn't write to his children, send them gifts or telephone them."

When Wills and Harry did spend time with Charles, it was often as hunting, fishing, or riding companions. The boys adopted their father's favorite pastimes. They also acquired a new nanny through their father: Tiggy Legge-Bourke. Charles had hired the young and attractive nanny to be with the boys when they were visiting him. The boys quickly took to Tiggy—and just as quickly Princess Diana did not! Some close to the family claimed that Diana was jealous of the close relationship Tiggy was developing with Wills and Harry. Others felt that the nanny was just another obstacle Diana found the Royal Family was putting in her way.

However, as much as Charles and Diana were privately disagreeing about their future together, they remained determined to ensure Prince William's continual training as a King of England. So, besides his educational studies, William was also learning the customs and proper behavior at royal ceremonies and appearances. His first official appearance was on March 1, 1991, when he participated in an event at Cardiff, the capital of Wales. He had to unveil a plaque in Cardiff at a ceremony that was to promote the city's history and commerce opportunities. That part was simple, but afterward, Wills had to greet the public. He shook hands with what seemed like thousands of people, smiled at their comments, and even had his cheek kissed over and over.

The Official Separation

In 1992, things came to a head on the Charles and Diana front. After months of headlines about their

Harry and William with their favorite nanny, Tiggy Legge-Bourke.

Diana, Charles, and Harry drop off William for his first day at Eton. The young Prince is in the care of House Master Dr. Andrew Gailey.

disintegrating relationship, their official separation was revealed. Actually, it was announced. Then British Prime Minister, John Major, gave a carefully worded statement as he addressed the House of Commons. In it he said the separation was amicable, that no divorce was imminent, and that the Prince's and Princess's official duties would not be affected.

Diana had already given the bad news to Princes William and Harry. She had gone to Ludgrove, where Harry had joined Wills, and told them privately so they wouldn't be upset by the news reports that would naturally result. Unfortunately, if Diana and Charles had thought a final announcement would quiet things down and make it easier for their boys, they were sadly mistaken.

In the months leading up to their official separation they had become known as the "Warring Wales." Charles's friends, and reportedly even the Palace, had leaked embarrassing tidbits about Diana to the press, while the Diana supporters pilloried Charles for his coldness as a husband and father. Charles was criticized for his seemingly uncaring attitude about Diana's dangerous bouts with depression and the eating disorder bulimia. And it seems every indiscreet comment Diana ever uttered was taperecorded or revealed by a former "friend." Reportedly, the final break came when Charles had scheduled an official family weekend at Sandringham. The high point of the weekend was to be a hunt. Diana

William with his school chums at Eton.

ETON FACTS

• Eton is a public school—in Great Britain that means it's a private school and not supported by the government.

• Eton is an all-boys school with an enrollment of about 1,200 to 1,300. It is a five-year school, equivalent to America's junior high and high school.

• Eton was founded in 1440.

• Eton's tuition is 13,000 pounds (about $20,000) a year.

• Eton's classes are divided into five "blocks"—during your first year, you are in F Block and finally in your last year, you are in B Block. There is no A Block anymore.

• Eton students all board—there are no day students. And students must spend every weekend at school during semesters at school.

• Eton has twenty-six "houses," or dorms. Each house has a headmaster, who handles the discipline of the boys and financial affairs and a dame, who handles the domestic areas of the house.

• Eton's nickname for a teacher is "Beak." However, when an Etonian refers to a specific teacher, he uses the teacher's initials. (For example, Prince William would refer to Headmaster Andrew Gailey as "AG.")

• Eton's uniform costs about $3,000 a year.

• Some famous Eton grads are King Henry VI, Sir Henry Wotton, Thomas Gray, Horace Walpole, Earl Spencer, and the Duke of Wellington.

had never been into the sport of hunting—she was an advocate of stopping cruelty to animals—so she decided not to go. As a matter of fact, she said she would really like to take the boys and spend the weekend with the Queen at Windsor or at their country palace, Highgrove. Reportedly, Charles was very upset and decided then and there to separate.

The Palace had hoped that with the announcement of their separation, the raunchy headlines and public backbiting would end. It didn't. As a matter of fact, it took on a whole *new* life. Diana's popularity seemed to grow as Charles was being blamed for the split. There were even those who called for Charles to abdicate his

right to the throne and pass the succession directly on to Prince William. The battle raged on.

Life Goes On

Meanwhile, Prince William was trying to lead the normal life of a young boy. In June of 1995, Prince William graduated from Ludgrove. Since Ludgrove is the pre-prep school for Eton College (the equivalent of high school in the U.S.), it was assumed that William would attend Eton. Of course, he had to take a difficult entrance exam. A strenuous slew of tests (there are twelve stages), the Eton

exam has been a stumbling block for many who wanted to attend the proud and exclusive school. Not so for William—he placed in the top half of his class on the exam and entered as an official Eton student in September 1995.

American writer Paul Watkins, who attended Eton, wrote about William's school choice: "Eton is extraordinarily well suited for a boy like [William]—a boy who has a public future. He must make his name within the school. He can't flex his money. There is no personal expression through clothes, and cars are not allowed. Wealth and status outside the school means little. He isn't even the only one at the school with a bodyguard! William is as near to

Prince William takes the oars at a rowing competition at Eton.

> *"Eton is extraordinarily well suited for a boy like [William]—a boy who has a public future....He isn't even the only one at the school with a bodyguard!"*

normal at Eton as someone in his position can be."

Established in 1440, Eton has long been regarded as one of England's best schools. There are some 1,200 to 1,300 students in total each year at Eton. Each year there are up to 250 new students accepted—in William's first year there were 240. William, along with forty-nine other boys aged fourteen to eighteen, was assigned to the ivy-covered dorm called Manor House. Indeed, some of William's Etonian newcomers were friends and classmates from Ludgrove, such as Andrew Charlton and Johnny Richards. Also assigned to Manor House was Nicholas Knatchbull, who was a year ahead of William, but was reportedly placed in the dorm to help the young prince adjust to his new surroundings.

Considering that William is the future King of England, there are those who think it might have taken a lot of "getting used to his surroundings." Instead of a suite fit for royalty, Prince William was given the normal ten-foot-by-seven-foot room where he would spend thirty-eight weeks of every year. There was a window, a single bed, a night stand, and a desk. The walls were to remain bare, devoid of posters and decorations. (However, it has been reported that William did pin up posters of some of his favorites, such as the Barbi Twins, Pamela Anderson Lee and Cindy Crawford!) The only thing that separated William from the other students was the fact that he had his own private bathroom and didn't have to share the communal bath and he did not have a plaque on the door with his name. That was for security purposes—as were the bodyguards assigned to stand outside his door.

Each dorm at Eton has a

Housemaster. At Manor House it was—and still is—Andrew Gailey. He and his wife, Shauna, have been at Eton for a number of years and those close to William say he developed a close relationship with them. They were there for him when his parents' marriage was dissolving, and later on when deeper tragedy struck the Royals.

When William first arrived at Eton, he threw himself into the routine wholeheartedly. The students wake up at 7:00 A.M. and dress in their Eton uniforms: a modified black swallowtail coat with black vest and pants and white button-down oxford cloth shirt. They have breakfast at 8:00. Then it is off to chapel service at 8:30. Daily classes begin at the stroke of 9:00 A.M. Students who are late for breakfast, chapel, or class must get up early the next day and sign a tardy book. If they have too many tardies, they are disciplined by losing privileges. After morning classes, the boys meet again in the dining hall for lunch at 1:30 P.M. After lunch, the boys go off to their respective sports—rugby, soccer, tennis, swimming at one of two pools, cricket, golf, and so on. Then, at 4:00 in the afternoon, classes start again, until dinner break.

Wills's Eton studies include

English; sciences such as chemistry, biology, and physics; history; music; and foreign languages such as Greek, Latin, and French. Also offered are electives such as studying the Swahili language or even cooking. But sports and academics are not the only areas emphasized at Eton. Spiritual and psychological counseling is also available to the boys. Britain has the highest divorce rate in Europe, and many of the boys at Eton are going through family splits. The teachers at Eton recognize that this can cause a lot of pressure for the students—and William is no different. As a matter of fact, London School of Economics professor David Starkey, another Eton graduate, observed: "William is as near to normal at Eton as someone in his position is wont to be. Many people there are richer than he is. There are many people whose family relationships are even far more complex than his."

Indeed, Eton soon became something of a protective island for William. There his life was regulated and disciplined—and protected. He was surrounded by friends and teachers who cared about him. Outside the walls of Eton, the battles could rage. Inside William was safe.

Even school work has to take second place when Prince William has royal duties.

Mum's Boy

"**M**ummy, I want to be a policeman so I can look after you," Prince William told his mother, Princess Diana, when he was very young.

Another time it was reported that a young Wills was so upset that his mother was in the bathroom crying that the little boy shoved tissues under the door and whispered to Diana, "I hate to see you cry, Mummy!"

Whatever Charles felt, whatever the Royal Family thought, not even *they* denied the fact that

Diana and Prince William enjoy a swim on a Caribbean vacation.

Prince William with his mother, Princess Diana, going to Christmas Day church services at Sandrigham.

Diana was an exceptional mother to William and Harry. She tried to be there for them all the time—partly to make up for the absences of their father, but most importantly because she adored her sons, whom she lovingly referred to as "My boys."

A Mother's Love

When Diana lived at Kensington Palace, the sitting room was practically a photo gallery dedicated to William and Harry. Though there were a number of "official" shots, most of the pictures were private photos of William and Harry. Framed photos from the time they were babies to their days at Ludgrove lined shelves and tables throughout the room. There were shots of the boys horseback riding, playing soccer or rugby, swimming in the Mediterranean, or just sitting and enjoying themselves—and many of the photos Diana had taken herself.

Diana's close friend and fellow charity enthusiast Lord Jeffrey Archer recalls the sitting room. "There are more pictures of [William and Harry] than of

anyone else. . . . She felt her life fell into two parts: her public, humanitarian side and the side where she was a mother."

Diana was a shining example when it came to both "sides" of her life, but motherhood was her driving force. Diana wanted William and Harry to enjoy as much a normal life as was possible in their unique position. Diana insisted that there were to be "fun days" as well as "work days" for the boys. On the fun days, Wills and Harry dressed in jeans, T-shirts, and baseball caps and hung out with their mom—they had lunch at McDonald's, went to amusement parks, and took in a movie. Diana was always giving her sons little surprises. Of course, as a Princess, "little" is a relative term. Take, for example, the time she arranged a tea at Kensington Palace with supermodel Cindy Crawford. William definitely had a crush on Cindy, and Diana wanted to give him a special treat. When Cindy first arrived at the Palace, she was ushered into a room where William was waiting. They were alone for a few minutes and chatted before Diana arrived. When she walked into the room,

Diana noticed that William was blushing, and she later whispered to Cindy, "He's just like me; when he runs out of things to say, he just blushes."

On work days, when the boys had to deal with their royal duties, they dressed in suits and ties and took on all their tasks with a maturity far beyond their years. But Diana didn't push them either. According to author Andrew Morton, she was determined they would be comfortable in all parts of their lives. "When they begin their public duties, they will be properly prepared. I don't want them suffering the way I did," Morton reports that Diana insisted.

When Wills had to deliver a short speech at a Christmas party Diana was hosting, she looked on proudly as he completed it flawlessly. "It was a polished performance," she later told friends.

But there were times Diana recognized that the boys were not ready for some duties. One of Diana's best friends, Tina Brown, former editor of the *New Yorker*, recalls a conversation they had shortly before the Princess's fatal car crash. It was about a decision Diana had to make about William accompanying his father on a very important ceremonial trip. Early in the summer of 1997, Hong Kong, which for decades had been ruled by the British, assumed self-rule. The British departure was to be heralded with much pomp and circumstance and Prince Charles was to head his country's delegation. "Charles suggested that [William] might go to Hong Kong [with him]," Tina says

Diana enjoyed this water park ride as much as Harry and William—and their bodyguard.

Diana told her. "But [William] said, 'Mummy, must I? I just don't feel ready.'"

William didn't go.

Lord Archer explained Diana's philosophy, especially with William. "She didn't want William to go through life thinking, 'You're a member of the Royal Family, and that's how you live all the time.' But she was particularly aware that William had his role to play, that she was the mother of the future King of England.

She was determined to introduce William, and Harry, to the responsibilities she knew someone of their status held—especially when it came to helping those who couldn't help themselves. Early on Diana had begun taking her boys along with her when she did charity work. She took them with her to visit AIDS patients and the homeless; she talked to them of her interests in getting medical and food supplies to areas of the world that needed them and of de-mining fields in war-torn areas across the globe.

"When you discover you can give joy to people...there is nothing quite like it," Diana told the *New Yorker*. "William has begun to understand that, too. And I am

Princess Diana instructs Prince William on his royal duties.

The Royal Family celebrates Prince William's Confirmation.

hoping it will grow in him."

Not surprisingly Diana hoped William would follow in the footsteps of another famous son: John Kennedy, Jr. "I'm hoping he'll grow up to be as smart about [life in the public eye] as John Kennedy, Jr.," she told friends. "I want William to be able to handle things as well as John does."

If William's actions are any example, Diana's wish has definitely come true. He has shown, in his own shy way, that he is accepting his royal responsibilities, but they are tempered with his mother's goodness and love. Those who are close to William agree with Harold Brooks-Baker, the publisher of *Burke's Peerage*. Says Brooks-Baker: "[Diana's] legacy of love will continue with William all the way to the throne."

The Divorce

Though Princess Diana and Prince Charles were separated at the time, they appeared with Princes Harry and William at the 50th Anniversary of the End of World War II.

On August 28, 1996, Charles and Diana were officially divorced. Actually, they could have cut their marital ties in 1994, since they had already fulfilled the two-year separation period decreed necessary by British law. When they didn't divorce right away, there were rumors that there might have been a reconciliation attempt. There were reports that Princess Diana had tried to enlist the aid of Queen Elizabeth in getting the couple back together. Insiders say that the Queen was all for it, but there was one sticky point: Camilla Parker-Bowles.

Princes William and Harry with their father, Prince Charles, at Balmoral shortly before Princess Diana's death.

Prince William makes sure his great-grandmother, the Queen Mother, enjoys her 97th birthday in August 1997.

According to many of Diana's friends, Camilla Parker-Bowles had *always* been a sticky point in the marriage of Diana and Charles. Camilla Parker-Bowles and Charles had been close for years and years. She actually had been Charles's first real love, and though they didn't marry, they kept a close relationship—even

after he married Diana. And it wasn't a secret. Diana often told her friends how much Charles's "friendship" with Camilla bothered her. She even took to calling Camilla "The Rotweiller." Though the dog reference may have sounded a bit catty, it was very obvious that Camilla didn't hold a candle to Diana's beauty and charm. In fact, Camilla was more like Charles. She had always been an outdoors woman, more interested in riding, hunting, and hiking than balls and parties. She was definitely someone who shared a lot of common interests with Charles. When Charles and Diana separated, he resumed seeing Camilla openly, especially after she divorced her husband.

The End of a Fairy Tale

There are those who insist that Diana would have reconciled with Charles if he agreed to break off completely any relationship with Camilla. Even the Queen agreed. But Charles didn't, so divorce was the only answer.

The irony is that Charles's

decision to keep a relationship with Camilla and end his marriage to Diana perhaps made the Princess even more popular. The public saw her as the devoted mother and loving wife who had tried her best to make things work. But Charles's distant manner, his sometimes even public humiliation of Diana, made many not so fond of their would-be King. Consider, for example, an incident back in 1991, when the couple hadn't yet officially separated, but the strain was already showing. They were at a polo match and Diana sat on Charles's precious Aston Martin car. Photographers and reporters who were all in hearing and photo range saw Charles turn to his wife and gruffly tell her not to sit on his $80,000 vehicle. "Get off, you'll dent the bodywork," he reportedly growled.

Needless to say, Diana was embarrassed and the tabloid journalists and photographers were quick to report the altercation. Numerous incidents such as these made the British public forgive any mistakes Diana might have made, and pulled her closer to their hearts. Indeed, because of the divorce, Diana may not have been in line to become Queen of England, but by 1996 she was already dubbed England's "Queen of Hearts."

It is the rare divorce that is simple, but there was *never* any thought that Charles and Diana's official split would be as easy as one-two-three. However, it was hardly money that was the problem in their divorce. No matter what, Diana would always be an extremely wealthy woman—after all, she was the mother of the "Heir and the Spare." But Diana was interested in more important things than cash, jewelry, and estates. She wanted to ensure her place in her children's lives and keep some of the influence and prestige she had

Diana insisted that she and Charles would both be involved in all decisions about William and Harry.

fought to have. As the Princess, Diana had grown from a shy, naive schoolgirl into a woman who understood that she could use her fame, power, and celebrity to help others. She didn't want to give that up.

First of all, Diana insisted that in the future, she and Charles would both be involved in all decisions about William and Harry. There was a chance that

Charles could just swoop in and take the boys away from Diana. By British law, he had the right to do that. According to the editor of *Majesty* magazine, Ingrid Seward, if Charles wanted to take complete custody of the boys, there was nothing Diana could do. "The boys belong to the Royal Family, not her," Seward explained about the royal custom.

Charles agreed, though there

Prince William with his cousins Zara and Peter Phillips.

are those who believe he did so reluctantly and only because popular opinion was with Diana. He also gave her a huge financial settlement, reportedly worth around $23 million. She kept her residence at Kensington Palace, and obviously had use of many of the other royal palaces when with her boys. She kept the jewelry she had been given over their fifteen year marriage, but she did give up some of the royal extras such as palace bodyguards and chauffeurs. Of course, with $23 million Diana could well afford to hire her own!

The other important concession Charles gave into was to have the Palace allow her to keep the title Diana, Princess of Wales. She did, however, give up the title's "HRH" (which stands for "Her Royal Highness") since she would now never become Queen of England. That was all fine and good with Diana. She had her children, could live comfortably and continue to be something of an ambassador to the world for her many charity causes.

William and Harry take a walkabout on the grounds of Balmoral with their father, Prince Charles.

Life After Charles

Though there were a number of scandalous headlines about extramarital relationships for both Charles and Diana during their separation, it seemed to many that the Princess picked all the wrong men. Forget about Charles! Among the millionaires, military officers, and playboys with whom Diana was linked, she seemed always to come up with her heart broken or her trust trampled on. James Gilbey, for example, was an ex-car salesman who published secretly recorded phone conversations with Diana, which even revealed his pet name for her—"Squidgy." There were rumors that she had a passing interest in one of her bodyguards, Barry Manakee, who was transferred from his post with her and later was killed in a motor-cycle accident. According to the tabloids, Diana even was linked romantically with King Juan Carlos of Spain! There were reported liaisons with banker Philip Dunne, cavalry major David Waterhouse, cavalry major James Hewitt, art dealer Oliver Hoare, British rugby star Will Carling, Pakistani heart surgeon Hasnat Khan, America billionaire Teddy Forstmann, and a number of others.

Of these men, Gilbey was not the only "friend" To turn on Diana. The one who probably hurt her the most was Major James Hewitt. He was Diana's riding instructor and when the Gulf War broke out, Hewitt went off to battle. When he returned to England, Diana and Charles were

Princes Harry, Charles, and William enjoy a holiday at Klosters.

just about to be officially separated. It was a good time for Diana. Friends say she and Hewitt had fun together. They enjoyed going out dancing, riding, and just laughing. Unfortunately Hewitt turned his relationship with Diana into $4.7 million betrayal—he wrote a tell-all book and revealed some very intimate memories in its pages.

Obviously Diana was hurt by this callous act, but more importantly she was worried about her sons. Both William and Harry were getting to be of the age that they heard and saw things on TV or in the papers. And even if they

were protected from headlines and sound-bites, they were surrounded by schoolmates who sometimes would tease them about their parents. By 1996 Diana was determined to protect her children, but she also wanted to get on with her life. She wanted to fall in love with someone who loved her back—and someone who would love and cherish her sons as much as she did.

That's when Dodi Al-Fayed came into Diana's life.

Time Together

On this Jet Ski romp William and Harry were wearing safety helmets —bet Diana had something to do with that!

Dodi Al-Fayed was the forty-one-year-old son of Mohamed Al-Fayed, a billionaire businessman who owned London's most famous department store, Harrod's, the Fulham soccer club, the Ritz Hotel in Paris, and many other businesses. Mohamed Al-Fayed had been a longtime close friend of Diana's father, Earl Spencer. Shortly before the Earl died, he had asked Mohamed to look after Diana. Though their lives rarely crossed—Mohamed Al-Fayed is not liked by the British upper

crust—the billionaire kept true to his promise to the Earl. Indeed, Diana and Mohamed did like each other and over the years she joined him and his family for special events.

In July 1997, Mohamed Al-Fayed invited Diana and her sons to join his family for a holiday at their villa in Saint-Tropez. One of his yachts was docked just off the coast, and Diana, William, and Harry took advantage of the clear blue water and fun in the sun. For one of the few times in her life, Diana did not seem to mind the ever-present photographers. And they snapped picture after picture: Diana, William, and Harry swimming in the beautiful Mediterranean or jet skiing off the Al-Fayed villa's beach. There were shots of her standing next to a dark young man on the deck of the yacht and photos of her frolicking with William and Harry. The only time she got at all bothered by the paparazzi was when a boatload of them got too close to William and Harry. She asked them to back off a bit because William "gets really freaked out."

But then, she did throw out a tasty morsel another time as she teased some of the press. "Expect a big surprise with the next thing I do," she said.

None of the reporters had a clue that Diana's surprise was to go public with her relationship with Dodi Al-Fayed. According to friends, they had been quietly seeing each other for at least six months. There are those who insist Diana and Dodi were very serious about each other, that this family vacation not only established their romance, but also Dodi's affection for Wills and Harry. While in Saint-Tropez, the boys seemed like regular kids—with Dodi, Diana, and other members of the party they went to an amusement park, where they had a great time crashing bumper cars into each other, and they stopped by pizza joints for a slice, and went shopping for souvenirs.

A New Beginning

Later that month, Diana and Dodi returned to the Mediterranean for another short vacation. This time it was just the two of them and they were taking a cruise on another one of the Al-Fayed

Prince Harry tears up the waters off Saint-Tropez in his Jet Ski.

Diana enjoys fun in the sun with William and friends in Saint-Tropez.

yachts, the *Jonikal*. But it wasn't until one entrepreneurial photographer—with a zoom lens—followed the Al-Fayed yacht as it cruised off Sardinia, that things exploded. With one quick snap of the lens, what had been private soon became worldwide news. Diana was photographed kissing Dodi Al-Fayed on the yacht. The photo soon became known as "The Kiss" and earned the lensman quite a bundle!

Amidst all the hubbub, Diana remained fairly calm. She even went about her regular routine after she returned from the cruise. She traveled to Bosnia to publicize her work at banning and clearing all land mines. In Sarajevo and Tuzla she visited with survivors of land-mine explosions and brought to the world's attention a horror few even knew about. But even as Diana performed her works of charity, she was in constant touch with Dodi.

Then, toward the end of August, while William and Harry were spending some vacation time

William gets some last minute advice from Diana as he roars off on his Jet Ski.

with their father at Balmoral, Diana joined Dodi one more time in Saint-Tropez and on the yacht. This time, the paparazzi had gotten out of hand and were stalking the couple in low-flying helicopters over the villa and yacht. The Al-Fayed family was quite upset, and on August 29, Dodi and Diana decided to cut their vacation short and fly to Paris for a romantic night. The day after, Diana was to join William and Harry to get them ready to go off to school.

The next day, August 30, Dodi and Diana boarded his private jet and flew from Sardinia to Paris. Once they arrived in the City of Light, they went to Dodi's Paris residence, then left for dinner at the Ritz Hotel. It has been reported that during that time, Dodi asked Diana to marry him and presented her with a magnificent emerald-cut diamond ring he had designed just for her at the exclusive Repossi Jewelers. Those close to Dodi say the gift, worth $205,400, was to be an engagement ring for Diana.

No one will ever know the entire story because after an intimate private dinner at the Ritz, Dodi and Diana quickly left for Dodi's home. In an effort to fool the stalking paparazzi, they changed cars and drivers and zoomed away from the back of the hotel. Still, they were discovered by the paparazzi and followed by a slew of them on motorbikes. Minutes later, the Mercedes S-600 limo that had been carrying Diana, Dodi, bodyguard Trevor Rees-Jones, and driver Henri Paul, lay in a massive, tangled wreck in the middle of the tunnel under the Place de l'Alma Bridge. Paul had lost control of the speeding limo and smashed into the thirteenth pillar in the tunnel and then careened off the wall. At shortly after midnight of August 31, 1997,

Dodi and Paul lay dead. Diana was dying and the only one eventually to survive was Rees-Jones (he was the only one who had his seatbelt on).

An emergency call rang at the police department at 12:27 A. M. and an ambulance arrived some fifteen minutes later. Dr. Frederic Maillex was the first doctor on the scene and at first he did not

recognize Diana as the severely injured woman in the back seat of the car. When the emergency paramedics finally were able to extract Diana from the wreck, she was taken to Salpetriere Hospital, where she died after heroic attempts to save her life.

For many the fairy tale finally ended that night. There would be no more happily ever after.

William gets scuba diving instructions during their Saint-Tropez vacation.

The Day the World Cried

*Prince William stops to read some
of the notes left in the floral
offerings in honor of his mother.*

I

n the hours and days immediately after Diana's death, it looked as if there would be no more happiness in the kingdom. The bulletin of Diana's death flashed all over the world, and it seemed the entire population of Earth sat in stunned silence listening to TV and radio reports. William and Harry were with their father at Balmoral and he had the excruciating duty to tell his sons that their mother had been killed in an accident.

Charles's next duty was no less demanding. He flew to Paris to escort Diana's body back to England.

Prince William in the funeral procession for his mother, Princess Diana.

Princess Diana's casket with the Royal Guard.

Along with her sisters, Sarah and Jane, the Prince accompanied Diana on her last trip home.

For William and Harry the following days must have seemed like a ghostly daze. For Great Britain it seemed as if time had stopped. Even before the entire Royal Family had returned to England, the flowers, gifts, personal notes, and offerings began to mount up in front of Kensington Palace, Buckingham Palace, and other places connected to Diana. Partly due to the nation's outcry, Queen Elizabeth ordered the British flag to fly half-mast over Buckingham Palace. This was not traditional because Diana was no longer a member of the Royal Family and the flag only flies when the Queen is in residence—but the love of the people, who had taken to calling her "Queen of Hearts," demanded it.

On Friday, September 5, Queen Elizabeth spoke to the nation in a live televised address from the Chinese Dining Room at Buckingham Palace. In part she said:

> First, I want to pay tribute to Diana myself. She was an exceptional and gifted human being. In good times and bad, she never lost her capacity to smile and laugh, nor to inspire others with her warmth and kindness. I admired and respected her—for her energy and commitment to others, and especially for her devotion to her two boys. This week at Balmoral, we have all been trying to help William and Harry come to terms with the devastating loss that they and the rest of us have suffered.
>
> No one who knew Diana will ever forget her. Millions of others who never met her, but felt they knew her, will remember her. I for one believe there are lessons to be drawn from her life and from the extraordinary and moving reaction to her death. I share in your determination to cherish her memory. . . .

A Last Good-bye

On September 6, 1997, millions watched as Diana's family, friends, and grieving public said their farewells at her funeral. The procession went from Diana's home at Kensington Palace to Westminster Abbey, where the funeral service was performed. A cortege carried the casket, on which lay three wreaths of white roses, lilies, and tulips. They were from William and Harry and Diana's family. But the most moving offering was a white card encased in the flowers that read simply, "Mummy."

William and Harry—along with their father, Prince Charles; their grandfather, Prince Philip;

and their uncle, Diana's brother Earl Spencer—joined the procession at St. James Palace and walked behind the cortege. Following them were representatives of many of the charitable organizations Diana worked with. There were people with AIDS, members of the Red Cross, a contingent from homeless charities, as well as survivors of land mines, many of whom were in wheelchairs.

When they arrived at Westminster Abbey, the crimson-uniformed Welsh Guard carried the casket inside the most revered place of worship in Great Britain. Though there were cameras recording the whole ceremony, the Royal Family had requested that no one go out of their way to film, videotape, or photograph the boys' faces. They were due their time of grief.

The service included Anglican hymns and prayers; a reading from Prime Minister Tony Blair, who considered Diana a good friend; poems read by Diana's sisters, Lady Sarah McCorquodale and Lady Jane Fellows; and a tender, but at times biting eulogy by her brother, Earl Spencer. In a full voice, heavily laced with emotion, Diana's brother touched on the best and the worst moments of Diana's life. Pointing a finger at the

"…today [we] pledge ourselves to protecting [Diana's] beloved boys, William and Harry…"

paparazzi who haunted her day and night, Earl Spencer laid blame, but in the next breath he pledged that he, his family, and even the entire nation would look after Diana's cherished sons, William and Harry. He said, in part:

> It is a point to remember that of all the ironies about Diana, perhaps the greatest is this: that a girl given the name of the ancient goddess of hunting was, in the end, the most hunted person of the modern age.
>
> She would want us today to pledge ourselves to protecting her beloved boys, William and Harry, from a similar fate. And I do this here, Diana, on your behalf. We will not allow them to suffer the anguish that used regularly to drive you to tearful despair. . . .

After the eulogy, Diana's good friend pop star Sir Elton John performed a special version of his song "Candle in the Wind." John and writing partner Bernie Taupin had written special lyrics for Diana—and the song, when later released, sold multimillions of copies, with much of the profits going to Diana's charities.

Finally, after all the pomp and circumstance, the family and close friends once again followed Diana's casket, this time in a two-

The floral tributes to Princess Diana.

hour car procession to Northamptonshire, for a private burial at Althorp, the Spencers' ancestral home.

From the Althorp estate, Charles brought William and Harry back to Highgrove, which would be their home. Charles even opened himself up to the British press and asked that they take a step back and leave William and Harry alone "so they can come to terms with their loss and prepare for the future."

Amazingly, the British press has cooperated—even to the present! But even with the press using kid gloves, it wasn't going to be an easy transition for William and Harry. Perhaps the most eloquent and insightful observation came from a peer of the boys, twelve-year-old Alexander Burrell. He is the son of Diana's butler Paul Burrell and a friend of William and Harry's. "I'm sure they are going through a lot of pain and sadness,"

Alexander said. "Your mum cares for you and looks after you. It's really sad for William and Harry that they won't have that. No one can replace her."

A Stiff Upper Lip

Just days after the funeral, William returned to Eton and Harry to Ludgrove for the fall 1997

Prince Charles comforts Princes William and Harry.

semester. It was decided that the boys should get back to a normal life as soon as possible. Of course, that was very difficult—especially since Harry turned thirteen on September 15, little more than two weeks after his mother's death. But Charles was determined to be there for his sons and help them deal with their grief. During Ludgrove's half-term break, Charles brought Harry on a State trip to Africa. Unfortunately, William couldn't go along because of his schedule at Eton. While Charles met with South Africa's president Nelson Mandela, Harry went on a three-day visit to a safari park in Botswana's Okavango Delta. Harry was allowed to bring one of his close friends, schoolmate Charlie Henderson. Charles also sent along the boys' much-loved nanny, Tiggy Legge-Bourke, to look after his charges.

After the safari, Harry met up with his father in Johannesburg. The highlight of that leg of the trip was a Spice Girls concert, at which Harry and his party went backstage to hang out with Scary, Ginger, Posh, Sporty, and Baby Spice! Harry's personal favorite Spice Girl, Emma "Baby Spice" Bunton, gave him a hug when the group greeted the royal party

Princes William and Harry bow as their mother's casket passes by on its way to Westminster Abbey.

backstage. Needless to say, Harry blushed a bright red, but once he finished posing for pictures, the thirteen-year-old prince turned back into a typical school boy. Said one observer, "Every now and again, Harry would look at his school chum and have a giggle."

Earl Spencer, Prince William, Prince Harry, and Prince Charles (left to right) flanked by priests who served at Princess Diana's funeral.

To many it seemed that Charles was truly trying to be there for his sons—not that he could ever make up for the loss of Diana, but just maybe he could make that awful transition easier. In that effort, Charles brought back Tiggy Legge-Bourke, not so much as a nanny to two teenage boys, but as a companion, a confidant, a friend. Author Brian Hoey was quoted in *People* magazine shortly after Diana's funeral: "[Tiggy Legge-Bourke] will be trying to shield [William and Harry] and calm them down. I feel sure she will come back much more closely into the fold. She draws them out and makes them laugh. . . . Tiggy will be a fixture in the Prince of Wales' household for the foreseeable future."

Tiggy definitely fits right in with the Wales men. "She's a country person, which the boys love," explains Santa Palmer-Tomkinson, a friend of Tiggy's. "She's one of the only women I know that can skin a rabbit or gut a stag."

When William is not at Eton and Harry is not at Ludgrove, they return home to Charles's royal residences Balmoral and Highgrove. This is fine with them because they both share their father's love of the outdoors, of riding and hunting and hiking. Also, it seems that William and Harry both prefer a life away from the prying eyes of reporters to enjoying the social whirl of the city. Judy Wade, royal reporter for the British magazine *Hello!,* observed: "Harry will feel Diana's loss most keenly. William can cope, he is more manly—he's had to be because he is the oldest son."

Another reporter, Richard Kay, who writes for Britain's *Daily Mail*, added: "William craves privacy. He is not a great lover of London life. Harry is growing that way too. When the boys were with their mother, they were hassled because of the paparazzi, but with their father, they're on the royal estates, they're undisturbed, and they find that blissful."

When the boys do spend time in London, it is at the newly refurbished York House at St. James Palace. After their mother's death, Charles had York House totally redone by interior decorator Robert Kime. According to those close to the family, York House is definitely teenage-boy friendly. There's a computer room, a pool table, and even a room for Tiggy Legge-Bourke.

As for the rest of William and Harry's family, they all have been as attentive and caring as they could be. Aunts Lady Sarah and Lady Jane visit the boys whenever they can. Their Uncle Charles, Earl Spencer, has lived in South Africa for a number of years, but he visited with Harry during his African visit and sees the boys whenever he is in England. There are rumors that he intends to move back to the Spencer' home, Althorp, and hopes to be a major presence in the boys' lives. And

Charles's side of the family has been there, too. His sister and brothers are always available to the boys. But it is Queen Elizabeth who has become the major female figure in their lives—especially in William's. More and more often William has been seen visiting his grandmother for tea at Buckingham Palace. Observed one British writer: "William could be the next king. . . . He knows what his destiny is. So the Queen . . . will be integral to his upbringing now."

Prince Philip, Prince William, Earl Spencer, Prince Harry, and Prince Charles (left to right) during Diana's funeral procession.

His Royal Sighness

Prince
William at
Balmoral.

By the time Prince William became a teenager, he was already a cover boy—not so much in the tabloid press, but in the teen press! British teen-zines such as *Smash Hits*, *Big!* and *Sugar* were covering Wills as if he were Leonardo DiCaprio or the Backstreet Boys. He was a superstar without ever appearing in concert or a movie or a TV series! British girls pulled out the Wills posters and pinups from the magazines and put them up on their walls and lockers.

Prince William shows off his "Roots Canadian-Olympic" jacket during his visit to Canada.

Prince Charles and Prince William go to service at Westminster Abbey.

The Royal Post Office was flooded with fan mail for Prince William. Though he tried to take it all in stride, Wills was somewhat mystified by the attention he was getting. But no matter what, the level-headed side of William ruled. When a reporter compared him to movie heartthrob Leonardo DiCaprio, William answered simply, "I think he'll find it easier being King of Hollywood than I shall being King of England."

William was right. Though Leonardo DiCaprio may be engulfed by fans when he makes a public appearance, celebrity is a choice he made. For William, it was a birthright and nothing he could ever do would change it. From the time he was born, the public wanted to know *everything* about him—his first step, first word, first tantrum. As a schoolboy, even his grades were of public concern. And when he lost his mother in a tragic accident, William's every step, tear, or comment was recorded for the ages.

The attention did not subside with the funeral of Princess Diana. Actually, the entire nation was concerned with how William and Harry would handle the first holiday after their mother's death. It was Christmas and usually a joyous time of year. For the Royal Family it was bittersweet. The official Christmas card from Prince Charles was a photo of him with William and Harry. They had posed for it only days before Diana's accident, so it brought back a flood of memories.

However, in true regal fashion, the Royal Family followed their normal traditions for the holiday. They stayed at the royal estate of Sandringham and went to the

Church of St. Mary Magdalene for Christmas services. In yet another irony, that was the church where Diana had been christened as a baby. In his holiday homily the minister, Canon George Hall, prayed for Diana, saying: "We thank God for those whom we love but see no more, Diana, Princess of Wales and all loved ones who have departed this life."

After the church service, the Royal Family followed tradition and met with the townspeople of Norfolk. An informal procession of local children presented the Queen and the Queen Mother with floral bouquets; Charles and the boys went for a "walka-bout"—a stroll around the area where they stopped and talked to their neighbors. Many gave William and Harry gifts, and they had a kind word for everyone.

With the Christmas holidays drawing to an end, William and Harry prepared to go with their father for their annual skiing trip to Klosters, Switzerland. They arrived at the exclusive ski area on December 31, New Year's Eve. The royal party—which included the boys' cousin, 16-year-old Zara Phillips, and Tiggy Legge-Bourke—stayed at the Walserhof Hotel in Klosters and celebrated the new year with a private

Cousin Zara Phillips joined Princes William, Charles, and Harry (left to right) for their winter vacation at Klosters in January 1998.

William schusses down the slopes at Klosters.

dinner, after which they watched a huge fireworks display that took place with the beautiful Alps as a backdrop.

The next day, the group hit the slopes and when Charles, Zara, William, and Harry spied a group of photographers, it went well—mainly because an arrangement had been struck between them and the royals' security people. The Royal Family would pose for photos for a short time, and then they would hit the slopes unimpeded by the press.

"The Prince of Wales recognizes the public's legitimate interest," a royal aide explained. "But they would then like to be left alone for the rest of their holiday. They don't expect to see a lens, camera, whatever, anywhere near them."

During the photo-op, Prince Charles joked with the press, describing the foursome, "We're the barbershop quartet." And after a short session, the group made for the ski lift. Later a royal aide commented happily, "They enjoyed a completely media-free day."

Prince Charles attends the premiere of Spice World *with his sons, William and Harry.*

A New Year

The next major public appearance by Prince William proved—to *anyone* who doubted—his appeal as teen idol. It was an official two-day tour of Vancouver, Canada, that would be capped by a vacation at a local ski slope. Prince Charles, accompanied by William and Harry (and Tiggy Legge-Bourke), arrived on March 23, 1998.

As the group arrived at each of their stops, they were greeted by thousands of young girls cheering. The headlines blared: "Wills Gets Young Hearts Racing!"..."Canadians Worship Princes of Hearts!"..."Prince William—Teen Dream!"

The Royal Family first stayed at the Waterfront Centre Hotel in Vancouver, and the sidewalks outside the front door were lined with some 8,000 Canadians. Young girls were crying out William's name, pushing bouquets of flowers at him. Some even offered him their phone numbers! William shyly smiled and was whisked into the hotel and quickly shown to their suite, which had been fully stocked with the boys' favorite chocolates, fruit, and CDs by Savage Garden, Oasis, and the Spice Girls. Sounds a bit like the backstage dressing rooms of rock stars!

Toni Dixon, a fourteen-year-old student who was at the hotel, told *People* magazine: "I was shaking, but [as William] walked by I held out my flowers. He looked into my eyes all the time and said, 'Thank you. It was nice to meet you.' It was so beautiful! Then I started bawling!"

Another female fan, seventy-year-old Bernice Moore, told the *Toronto Star* newspaper she had come because "I just had to see Diana's little boys."

The Royals at Christmas 1997 at Sandringham—William with cousin Peter Phillips and Serena Linley.

The reaction from the citizens was one thing, but once again it seemed the boys were surrounded by photographers and reporters. Before they had even left for Canada, Prince Charles had requested that the press go easy on the boys. But while most tried, it was almost impossible when you consider that some 300 reporters had come over from Europe just to cover the royal visit—and that's not even counting the Canadian press!

According to reporter Peter Archer, "[William] was unsettled by the welcome." Perhaps because of the push and shove of their reception, William requested that they call off the photo-op scheduled at their first official visit—the Pacific Space Centre museum. Free of prying eyes, they spent two hours in the Space Centre. William and Harry shot off rockets, played computer games, and even took a simulated Mars flight.

The second stop for the group was at the South Burnaby Secondary School. The press described the young high school students' behavior as reminiscent of the first time the Beatles arrived in North America. Girls

Prince William visits the Space Center in Vancouver, Canada.

were shaking with emotion, screaming, "Wills, we love you!" and even sobbing hysterically. Girls were chanting Wills's name and others were holding up teen magazines with Prince William on the cover.

When the party went inside the high school, they were treated to a performance by the school band. Then some students presented William with a Vancouver Grizzlies team jersey and Harry with a Canuck's hockey sweater.

As the day's appearances wound down, William seemed to be at ease. Perhaps it was because he was surrounded more and more by kids his age. The last official stop was at a Pacific Marine Heritage Legacy event at the Canada Place. Charles, Harry, and William were presented with official Roots Canada red-and-white Olympic jackets and matching "poor boy" hats. Much to the delight of the audience, all three donned the jackets, but Wills jumped in front, turned his hat backwards in street fashion and held his arms out, giving his dad a rapper-style salute! As Harry joined the audience in cracking up at Wills's antics, reporters were creating the next day's headline—"Fresh Prince With Street Cred!"

William and Harry—and presents—after the Christmas service at Sandringham.

Prince William says hello to students at Vancouver's Burnaby High School.

After that appearance, the Royals took off for their four-day ski trip at Whistler Mountain, some 60 miles from Vancouver. The three Princes—Charles, William, and Harry—all took separate helicopters, keeping with the royal rule that heirs to the throne should not fly together in case of an accident.

Unfortunately, the media began to get a little out of hand once the Royal Family was at Whistler. But for once, it reportedly wasn't the British press that breached the understanding of privacy Prince William had asked for. It was three Canadian crews from CBC, Global TV, and a Vancouver station, VTV. On the first morning of skiing for the princes, the TV crews had camped out at the chair lift at the foot of Blackcomb Mountain. They immediately began shooting as the princes arrived, and Prince Charles was quite upset. Mounties quickly moved in and pushed back the crews. A spokesperson for Buckingham Palace immediately issued a warning that if there were any more intrusions on the Royals' privacy, they would cancel the scheduled photo-op on the slopes. They also requested that any unapproved footage shot

Prince William jumps from the helicopter that took him from Vancouver to Whistler for a skiing vacation.

Prince William waves good-bye to the cheering crowd in Vancouver.

William the Conqueror

Of course, Harry could be learning a bit from his older brother. The younger prince might enjoy being something of a teen idol, too. But then, he'd better get used to the ribbing William gets from his cousins about his teen popularity. Cousin Zara Phillips has been with William many times when young girls approach him and start to giggle or stammer because they are so nervous. And Zara is a consummate tease! One day, she was with William when they were hosting a charity event and were mobbed by local students. One girl came up to William and pushed a flower toward him. He chatted with her briefly and she seemed ecstatic. Later on the royal cousins heard that a reporter had asked the girl about meeting William, and she responded, "I wanted to give him a kiss, but it happened so quickly. He seemed very shy!"

If that didn't declare Prince William the Prince Charming of Teen Idols, well, even American magazines have taken up the banner. *YM* had him on their

that morning not be aired. Ironically, many members of the British press urged their Canadian counterparts not to "screw up" The rest of the trip.

Obviously the warnings were heeded because after the unwanted intrusion, things went smoothly. William and Harry seemed really to relax, so much so that they began pelting their bodyguards with snowballs as they waited to get on the ski lift. Later on that day, when the family stopped at a restaurant on the slopes for lunch, both boys were smiling and laughing and joking with the other skiers. Harry even winked at a group of women who were waiting to be seated. Cheeky boy!

February 1998 cover and ran a two-part story on Wills in the February and March issues. Teen fanzines *SuperTeen*, *Teen Beat*, and *16* have run countless articles on the prince. But the ultimate compliment was paid by *People* magazine when they included Prince William in their special issue of the "50 Most Beautiful People in the World—1998."

The fact is that Prince William takes all this in stride. Though, according to author Brian Hoey, "The feeling among members of the royal household is that secretly he quite enjoys it," all the attention hasn't gone to Wills's head. It must be hard not to have an inflated ego with thousands of girls calling your name, but Prince William tempers that display of affection with the realization that he also has a job to do. That was always one of Princess Diana's concerns, but shortly before her death she told a reporter: "I try to din [it] into him all the time . . . how he must understand and handle it. I think he has it. I think he understands."

William does . . . and Diana would be proud. She did her job well.

Like his father, William likes getting back to nature at Balmoral.

Royal
Facts

The Royal Family in 1990.

What kind of security protection does Prince William have?
He wears an electronic tracking bracelet that keeps him in constant touch with Palace security. Prince William is also accompanied by two Scotland Yard detectives wherever he goes on his daily schedule.

Did Prince William have braces on his teeth?
Yes. He recently had them removed.

Is it true that Prince William is a computer whiz?
The Prince is quite computer literate and loves to e-mail family and friends. It has been reported that he even had the e-mail address of the President of the United States on his e-mail address book.

Does Prince William live in the dorm at Eton College?
Yes. He's treated as normally as possible. The only difference between Prince William's room and the other borders is that he doesn't have a nameplate on his door and he has his own bathroom. The other boys have to share communal bathrooms.

Prince William has been included in a number of "Best Of" lists—what are they?
The British press voted Prince William one of the "Top Ten Best Behaved People of 1997" because of his actions after the death of his mother, Princess Diana. American TV

Prince William inherited the shy smile of his mother, Princess Diana.

Those close to the Royal Family say that Prince William is very protective of Prince Harry. That's one of the reasons Harry will join William at Eton.

reporter Barbara Walters named him one of the "Top Ten Most Interesting People of 1997." And *People* magazine included Prince William in their "50 Most Beautiful People" of 1998.

Is it true that Prince William and Prince Charles are not allowed to fly together in the same airplane?

Yes. It is a protective measure to ensure that, if there were an accident, the succession to the throne would not be jeopardized.

Has he shown his artwork in a gallery?

Not yet, but one of his drawings of a stone house was displayed at an Eton Art Show.

What is Prince William's full name?

According to those who study genealogy, it would be William Arthur Philip Louis Schlesweig-Holstein-Sonderburg-Glucksburg-Saxe-Coburg-Gotha. However, Queen Elizabeth II decided some time ago to shorten the family name to Mountbatten-Windsor. Mountbatten is the family name of her husband,

Prince Philip, and Windsor is the official surname of her line of British royalty.

Could Prince William marry an American and still become King?

According to the British Act of Settlement of 1701, those who are in direct line of succession to the throne may not marry a Roman Catholic or a divorced person. That is because the British monarch also holds the title of Defender of the Faith of the Church of England. As for marrying an American, or any other nationality, there are no specific rules against it, but British public opinion might influence a monarch's choice.

Did Prince Harry buy a girl a present while he was on his African trip?

Yes—a Zulu bracelet for "nanny" Tiggy Legge-Bourke.

Did William answer the condolence letters he received after his mother's death?

William and Harry received hundreds of thousands of letters from people all over the world, so it would have been physically impossible to answer them all. They actually have answered the letters from people they know and made public statements of thanks for the others.

Charles used to read stories to William and Harry. What were they?

They were the works of Rudyard Kipling, such as *The Jungle Book*.

Did William win a swimming event at Eton?

Yes. according to the British newspaper the *Sun*, early in 1998: "The 15-year-old showed he has inherited mother Diana's swimming skills by winning the school's junior 100-meter and 50-meter freestyle finals. Wills, who trains in the pool three times a week, clocked 1 minute, 02.84 seconds in the 100-meter race and 27.94 seconds in the 50-meter dash."

Is Prince William conceited?

No. Says royal watcher and author of thirteen books on the Windsor family, Brian Hoey, "He's unselfconscious about his physical attributes."

Is it true that Prince William wants the Diana, Princess of Wales Memorial Fund to close down?

The London *Sunday Times*

According to Diana's close friend, Lord Archer, she felt Prince William "had all the right qualities to be a monarch."

reported that the Prince is "angry and upset" over the sometimes tasteless commercialization that has come about in the name of this charity. Though a proposed official Diana underwear was turned down, the Fund has approved official Diana teddy bears and lottery tickets—and even margarine. Those close to William say newspaper reports about the Fund disturb William because they bring back too many memories.

Royal Stats

The Basics

Full Name: William Arthur Philip Louis Mountbatten-Windsor

Nicknames: Will, Wills, Wombat, Dreamboat Willie, Billy the Basher

Official Title: His Royal Highness Prince William of Wales

Future Title: King William V of Great Britain

Birthdate: June 21, 1982, at 9:03 P.M.

Birthplace: St. Mary's Hospital in Paddington, London

Birth Weight: 7 pounds, 10 ounces

Astrological Sign: Gemini, on the cusp of Cancer

No one would have guessed how the Royal Family's story would have turned out when this photo was taken.

*Prince William
smiles more now that
he got his braces off!*

Princes Harry and William are joined by cousins Princesses Eugenie and Beatrice at Klosters in 1995.

Christening: August 4, 1982, in the Music Room, Buckingham Palace

Parents: Prince Charles and the late Princess Diana

Sibling: Prince Henry "Harry" Charles Albert David Mountbatten-Windsor

Paternal Grandparents: Her Majesty Queen Elizabeth II and the Duke of Edinburgh, Philip Mountbatten

Maternal Grandparents: Frances Shand-Kydd and the late Earl of Spencer

Royal Great-Grandparents: The Queen Mother, Elizabeth Bowes-Lyon, and the late King George VI

Height: 6' 2"

Weight: 130 pounds

Hair: Blond

Eyes: Blue or hazel—it depends on what he's wearing

Righty or Lefty? William is left-handed

Primary Current Residences: St. James Palace in London until Prince Charles's new estate, Althorp House in Highgrove, is ready. While at Eton College, Prince William stays in Manor House.

Pets: Widgeon, a black Labrador

Instrument Played: Piano

Most Endearing Habit: He blushes when he gets unwanted attention.

Current Passion: Cars

Schools:
Mrs. Mynors's Nursery School (1985–1987)
Wetherby School (1987–1990)
Ludgrove School (1990–1995)
Eton College (1995–present)

Nursery School Lunch Box: Postman Pat

Childhood Pony: Trigger—he competed in his first horse show in 1988 and won third place.

Will has become quite a Jet ski daredevil.

Childhood Collections:
Transformers

Description by *Smash Hits***:**
"He's definitely ideal boyfriend material," states the top British teen mag, which has often run covers and posters of Wills.

Wills's Faves

Sports: Rugby, swimming, tennis, horseback riding, shooting, water polo, skiing, rowing (called sculling at Eton), and hockey

Music: Techno

Musical Groups: Oasis, Pulp, Spice Girls

Pastimes: Video games, mountain biking, reading classic literature and poetry

Drink: Coke

Food: French fries, pizza, pasta, fruit salad, free-range eggs, vegetables, and venison

Boxers or Briefs? Prefers boxers, but wears both

Childhood Play Place: Windsor Safari Park

Childhood Excursion: The zoo

More royal duties for Harry and William.

Getaway Place: Scotland

Vacation Places: Klosters, Switzerland (for skiing), Eleuthra in the Caribbean (for sun and surf), and Disney World in Orlando, Florida

Hobbies: Hunting, painting

School Subjects: French and art

Model: Cindy Crawford—his mother, Princess Diana, once arranged a tea at the Palace for Cindy and Will.

Spice Girl: Emma "Baby Spice" Bunton

Actress: Pamela Anderson—he had a poster of her on the wall of his dorm room his first year at Eton.

Dislikes
• Tabloid press
• Paparazzi
• Champagne
• Red meat
• Mobile phones

Where to Write Prince William

HRH Prince William
St. James Palace
London SW1A 1BS
Great Britain

Note: No mail will be accepted at Eton College.

Though Prince William is a strong rower, he prefers being behind the wheel of his go-cart or mountain bike. He'll get his driver's license when he turns 17.

"*William craves privacy. He is not a great lover of London life.*"

Prince William plays
with his dog, Widgeon,
at Balmoral.